REInventing
Ralph

A Little Story for Salespeople
About Culture-Driven
Selling

For John From John (handwritten inscription)

John Waid

INDIE BOOKS
INTERNATIONAL

Copyright © 2018 by John Waid

All rights reserved.

Printed in the United States of America.

No part of this publication may be reproduced or distributed in any form or by any means without the prior permission of the publisher. Requests for permission should be directed to permissions@indiebooksintl.com, or mailed to Permissions, Indie Books International, 2424 Vista Way, Suite 316, Oceanside, CA 92054.

Neither the publisher nor the author is engaged in rendering legal, tax or other professional services through this book. The information is for business education purposes only. If expert assistance is required, the services of appropriate professionals should be sought. The publisher and the author shall have neither liability nor responsibility to any person or entity with respect to any loss or damage caused directly or indirectly by the information in this publication.

ISBN-10: 1-947480-19-7

ISBN-13: 978-1-947480-19-3

Library of Congress Control Number: 2018941067

Designed by Joni McPherson, mcphersongraphics.com

INDIE BOOKS INTERNATIONAL, LLC
2424 VISTA WAY, SUITE 316
OCEANSIDE, CA 92054

www.indiebooksintl.com

Contents

Preface

This is a little story about a big idea in selling.

The day of process-laden selling models has run its course, as these models have been launched and forgotten by millions of people who went through a one- or two-day program and then left, only to go back to their old habits. By the way, enterprise investments in these process models are now in the billions of dollars, yet they are not working for most organizations or salespeople. Great selling is about great habits, and the process models do not do this requirement justice. The best salespeople do not sell; they help people to buy and have built values and behavior around this. Selling is not the action. *Buying* is. Think about it; even the best salesperson does not sell anything unless someone buys. Buying is the act, not selling.

In this story, Ralph, a salesman in his thirties who has come up on some really bad times at work and home, discovers three transcendent values. He helps to discover and climb Culture Mountain and become a winning, culture-driven salesperson.

No matter at what level you are in sales, you can never underestimate the power of simplicity and a mentor who understands you. A trusted advisor can make a big difference if the pupil is willing to learn. Ralph's mentor is David, and he and David create a bond that takes them from crisis to character and from the bottom of the barrel to the top of the line. This rags-to-riches tale will inspire you to conquer the Neanderthal in you and make awareness a power no one can stop.

"Culture eats strategy for breakfast," so leave the old sales processes behind and join Ralph on a journey of self-discovery. My hope is this book will do the same for you.

John Waid

Founder, C3—Corporate Culture Consulting

January, 2018

Chapter 1
Up or Out

Ralph arrived at the plant to meet with his boss, only to find he couldn't get through the gates. He had to park his dirty, red Ford F150 at a parking lot two blocks away. Ralph thought, "This always happens to me. It must be because my name is Ralph."

Man, it was hot, humid, and stagnating on that infernal August day in Columbia, South Carolina. Within minutes of starting the walk toward the plant, the sweat stains were visible from a mile away. Ralph was struggling to do anything right these days. His daughter, Becky, had yelled at him earlier that morning because she said he didn't understand her. Becky and the meeting with the boss would make for a bad day for poor Ralph, but that wasn't all. Rachel, his wife, had said she thought he was cheating on her because Ralph's coworker Linda kept calling him and he had gone into another room to talk with her. To add insult to injury, the pet cat had also scratched Ralph's face that morning out of the blue—a scratch that looked like he might have gotten from a fight.

By now, Ralph had a cascade of sweat droplets rolling down his face as the blistering sun kept beating down on him. Despite the heat and the trouble at home, all Ralph could think about was that he had lost three key sales the week before because clients wanted discounts he could not give them. Ralph was not one to cut corners and had earned his stripes being ethical in a time when others had not. At one of the grocery store chains Ralph called on, the buyer had gotten a new boat; Ralph was pretty sure that had come from his main competitor. As Ralph looked down

at his watch, he sped up his pace so he wouldn't
be late for his appointment with his boss.

The security guard at the plant entrance stopped
Ralph at the gate to tell him that his sticker was
expired; that was why he couldn't get in and
had to park in the other lot. Ralph was meek
and mild with the guard and accepted what he
said. He knew that he was sure to be late if he
did not. Ralph then saw Linda, the only sales
representative who had worked for the snack
food company longer than him; she warned him
again, as she had the night before, how angry
the boss was at him. Linda said their boss, Mr.
Stark, was out for blood and Ralph's blood type
was a match. Linda had overheard Mr. Stark tell
his own boss, Mr. Anderson, that the quarterly
numbers were bad and someone was going to
be held accountable. Since Ralph had the worst
numbers on the team and Mr. Stark hated him,
he was prepared for his beatings-will-continue-

until-morale-improves attitude to come out in all of its glory.

Down the main hall in the plant offices, Ralph ran into Stuart Lane (or as Ralph referred to him, Stuart "Lame"). Stuart was a favorite of Mr. Stark and due to some lucky wins was probably going to win a big sales contest that month. Just to rub Ralph's face further in the mud, Stuart said to him "Hey Ralphie, I had the best month ever, and you're in last place." Stuart was bitter because he was only a sales representative, whereas Ralph was a senior sales representative who had been destined to become the manager—at least until Mr. Stark got the promotion.

The hallway down to Mr. Stark's office was lined with performance and employee-of-the-month awards. In previous years, Ralph had enjoyed seeing his salesman-of-the-year awards hanging in the hallway when he went to see his former manager. Ralph referred to this period as "The Glory Years."

Ralph had been in trouble with Mr. Stark before, mostly because he challenged him often; deep down inside, he knew he could never live up to the manager he'd had before. Ralph's previous manager, Sam, had been an incredible manager, even though at first Ralph had not initially thought so.

Sam had worked in sales in the snack foods business for his entire career and was one of the hardest workers Ralph had ever met.

When Ralph first met Sam and reported to him at age eighteen, during his first year of college at The University of South Carolina, he was a new route salesperson. It was Ralph's first "real" job for a "real" company. Ralph had worked all kinds of smaller jobs before, but none had compared to this one. When Ralph was hired, Sam reviewed three rules with him. The first: "If you hit or cuss at a customer, you're fired." The second: "If you fail to show up and do not call us or you don't finish your route, you're fired." The third: "If you do any truck or property damage and do not tell us, you're fired." Then Sam had said, "These are the three rules for working here. Are we clear?"

Ralph was so scared of Sam at that point, he just said, "Yes, sir."

Sam had a strange way of training people, Ralph remembered. The first day of work (and every day after that) started at 5:00 a.m. On Ralph's first day, Sam said, "I am going to train you today," and then asked, "Are you ready?" Ralph was really excited to start his first day until he heard what Sam said next. "Pretend I am not here, use your brain, and start working." Ralph did not know what to do and did not say a word. Ralph looked around at what others were doing, then went to grab a flatbed truck and started putting potato chip boxes on it, as they were. He turned to Sam, who asked, "Do you have the same route as the person in front of you?"

Ralph admitted he didn't, and Sam said, "Then how would you find out what to put on the truck if I wasn't here?" Ralph answered he would look for someplace where it might tell him what products to put on the truck. Sam said, "That sounds like a smart idea."

Ralph next went off in search of Colonel Terrance, the general manager who had worked with Sam to make the company one of the best distribution operations in the country. Ralph asked Col. Terrance where to find out what to put on his truck. Col. Terrance said to Ralph, "The route books are over there. Is Sam training you?"

Ralph laughed a nervous laugh and shouted "Yes!" over his shoulder while running back to see Sam. Ralph was so proud he had found the books—until Sam asked him to look at the book and use his brain again. That's when Ralph saw that he had grabbed the Wednesday book instead of the Monday book. Ralph ran back fast to get the Monday book so they could load up and head out on the sales route.

Sam asked Ralph a lot of questions throughout the day and did not lift a finger to help Ralph. Ralph was overwhelmed and made tons of mistakes. He forgot to put gas in the truck, and they ran out of fuel. He forgot to take a hand truck and had to hand-carry all the boxes into the stores in 100-degree heat. It took Ralph almost two hours to service the first store. Ralph was so frustrated with Sam that he felt like punching him in the face, but Ralph realized if he did, he would be fired, per the rules. When they returned to the warehouse at 2 am the following morning, Sam said to Ralph, "You have made all the mistakes possible, including ones I have never seen before. Congratulations. You are fully trained." Unfortunately, that backhanded compliment did not help Ralph's mood; he was incredibly tired, and he knew he was due back to the distribution center in three hours.

The next day, Ralph serviced a store the size of the one that had taken him two hours the day before in thirty minutes, with very few mistakes. In that moment, Ralph was extremely proud and, in a strange way, appreciative of Sam's unorthodox and weird training method—the same method he had so hated just a few hours before.

Ralph continued to do his routes the rest of the summer. Toward the end of the summer, a supervisor with the nickname "Big Jim" rode along to do a check ride. After a couple hours, Big

Jim asked how long he had been working at the company. When Ralph told him that he had been there a couple months, Big Jim looked confused and said, "No way. I have seen ten-year veterans not do as good a job as you." His next questions and Ralph's answer made them both laugh. "Who trained you?"

Ralph said, "Sam."

Big Jim said, "That explains it. Sam is really good, I don't know what he does to train people so well."

Ralph answered in a serious, louder tone with a smirk on his face, "He doesn't do *anything*." Both of them laughed like crazy, and Ralph knew to this day that Big Jim had no idea how true that was, and how profoundly effective Sam's training method was, and how Ralph's answer would be a closely-held secret for Sam and Ralph as they trained some of the best salespeople at the company through the years.

✱

As Ralph continued to walk toward Mr. Stark's office, he remembered Sam with a smile and then some tears. Sam had died of a massive heart attack about six months previously. Ralph and Linda had helped carry the casket. Sam was a hero to Ralph and many others, and now he was gone. Ralph missed Sam so much.

As Ralph walked into Mr. Stark's office, he was reminded of how much Sam had helped him throughout his career with the company and how little this new boss knew about him, his character, and the great culture Sam, Col. Terrance and others had built. Mr. Stark was the opposite of Sam; he was famous for throwing people under the bus. Ralph's body language always changed as he approached Mr. Stark's desk, and today it was even more hunched over, matching his face, which had defeat written all over it.

Mr. Stark said, "Take a seat."

So far, the best part of Ralph's day had been remembering Sam. This happy memory was replaced by a sobering awakening. Mr. Stark looked Sam up and down and said, "I am disappointed in you."

Ralph asked, "What are you disappointed about?"

The other man replied, "Your poor results, and even worse, your terrible attitude."

Ralph retreated in defeat and said, "I'm sorry."

Mr. Stark must have felt bad for Ralph. He said, "Ralph, I am sorry also, and unfortunately, I am putting you on a PIP—a performance improvement plan. You have forty-five days to dramatically improve your results, or we will have to let you go."

Ralph left Mr. Stark's office just in time to run into Stuart Lame, who clearly knew what had happened and said, "Up or out Ralphie; up or out."

Chapter 2
Forty-Five Days

R alph did not know what he was going to do. His home life was a mess, and now his work life was about to be over. Down and depressed, Ralph decided to call his friend Chip, who always had a great attitude and knew how to say just the right thing. As Ralph talked to Chip, it became apparent to Ralph that he needed to change, and that if he didn't, he would lose his marriage and his job, which he considered a career; he loved selling. Chip suggested that he and Ralph go play golf, drink some beer, and get a chance to relax and figure things out. Ralph thought that was a great idea and scheduled time to play the following day.

It was a beautiful Saturday morning, and Ralph and Chip joined another twosome as it was a busy day at the golf course and they were not allowing twosomes to play by themselves. Chip and Ralph met Carl and David. Carl and David from Augusta, Georgia looked like they were in their sixties. As Ralph and Chip got to talking with David and Carl, they found out Carl was a very successful golf cart salesman and David was a friend who had worked with Carl for years.

The third hole was a long par-five with lots of water and sand. Chip teed off first and hit a beautiful drive down the middle. Carl followed with another gorgeous shot. Ralph hit it in the woods on the left side, and David also hit it in that same direction. As Chip and Carl waited for David and Ralph, they got to talking. It turned out that they had mutual friends in common and hit it off.

Deep in the woods, David was helping Ralph find his ball when suddenly David fell as he tripped over a branch. Ralph helped him up and made sure he was OK. David said to Ralph, "Thank you for helping out, young man." David and Ralph finally found both their balls and hit decent shots to get out of the trouble. As the foursome finished the third hole, it was decided that Chip would ride with Carl as they continued to share stories and that Ralph and David would ride in the other cart.

For the next six holes, David and Ralph talked and so did Carl and Chip. Everyone was getting along until Ralph told David his situation at work. After that, David decided to return to the cart with Carl. They finished the round without much additional chatting. At the end of the round, Ralph wanted to know why David had so abruptly decided not to continue riding with him in the cart. Ralph decided he would invite everyone to a round of beers; Carl and especially David tried several times to politely decline. As Ralph kept insisting, he said the magic words that seemed to get David to rethink his retreat by saying, "I won't take no for an answer."

They all ordered Tecate beer, as David had shared he liked going to Mexico and had grown to enjoy this beer. As they talked, David turned to Ralph and said, "Why don't you call me this week and let's chat about your situation." Ralph got David's information and the group disbanded.

Ralph returned home only to find Rachel crying and his younger daughter, Becky, gone to a friend's house. Their oldest, Emma was already away at college, so they had the place to themselves.

As Ralph asked Rachel what was wrong, she proceeded to spill her guts to him. Ralph still had not told her about his work situation; he was still digesting it himself. That was the wrong move. It turned out that Linda had called the house looking for Ralph and had inadvertently mentioned that Ralph was possibly going to lose his job. She was calling to tell him about an uncle of hers who may be able to help. Ralph's wife confronted Linda about the affair she thought they were having, and after a long talk, decided she was wrong about the affair. But still, she was *really* mad at Ralph for not telling her about what had happened at work. Ralph's wife didn't understand why he was in trouble at work; he had been so successful in the past.

Ralph was overwhelmed by the conversation, and although he wanted to tell Rachel a word or two, he decided to just listen.

After the smoke had cleared a little in Ralph's house, he called Linda back to find out about her uncle. As Ralph talked to Linda, it was decided. Ralph and Rachel would go over to Linda's house and have dinner with her, her husband, and uncle.

On Monday, Ralph called his new friend from the golf course, David, and left him a message. Ralph was so fearful about the position he was in, he stayed clear of the office that day and instead did three sales calls. That night, he and Rachel went to Linda's house.

Linda lived in a nice neighborhood and had a beautiful home. As Ralph and Rachel entered the house, they were greeted by two beautiful young kids who were about to get ready for bed. As Ralph and Rachel sat down for dinner, Linda said that her uncle was running late and may not make it, as he had gone to California to see a client on Sunday and was just getting back to Augusta, then driving to Columbia.

The dinner was delicious. Ralph was disappointed that he did not get to meet Linda's uncle, whom Linda called before Ralph and Rachel left; the uncle decided to meet Ralph if he would drive to Augusta the next day.

Ralph left the house in the dark the following morning; the drive was a long one, and he arrived after a lovely sunrise at a pretty big breakfast place in a strip mall in Augusta called Sunrise Grill. Ralph was a few minutes early and sat down at the breakfast bar with a view of the short-order cooks and a lot of bacon and sausage on the grill. As Ralph ordered some coffee, he looked down the bar and saw David from the golf course. He got up and went over to David and they started talking. It turned out David was supposed to meet a friend of his niece's whose name was Ralph. He hadn't put two and two together. They both laughed, and David said, "Fate has a funny way of putting people who need each other together."

Ralph was a bit nervous, as now he was with David in a different context. Linda had mentioned he was a world-famous motivational speaker and sales guru who had even advised presidents of companies and countries as they negotiated and built very successful teams, companies, and nations. As Ralph and David talked about what a small world it was, David said to Ralph, "You know, I got turned off when you started to tell me about your situation at work. I thought you were just another deadbeat salesman who could not make his numbers." David had found out from his niece the whole story behind Ralph's rise and fall and had wanted to help before even knowing it was the same person from the golf course.

Before realizing this Ralph was golf-course Ralph, David had come here this morning as a favor for his niece Linda. David had even helped and coached Linda and seen how successful she had become. David was all about results and only liked working with winners (or, in this case, former winners). As Ralph ordered breakfast, David turned to him and asked, "Have you ever heard, 'Culture eats strategy for breakfast'?" David explained that was a famous quote by a management guru named Peter Drucker. Ralph was a little confused by the quote; David explained that even as they ate breakfast, it was the *culture* of the breakfast place that made it so successful, and not just the *process* of how the employees made the breakfast or the *strategy* of offering a good breakfast to Augustans at a convenient location and a fair price. David explained how the restaurant handpicked the staff, made sure they all smiled, made the experience friendly, and made you feel at home. "They serve the same things other breakfast places serve; they just have a soul, and we call that soul 'culture,'" David explained.

Suddenly, David became stern in his demeanor. This was the same behavior Ralph had seen at the golf course. Ralph was unsettled. David explained that Ralph needed to give him $2,000 a week if he was going to help him and that if he were not willing to do this, he would not help him. David said if you are really serious about something, you need to put your money where your mouth is and be willing to work hard if you intend to climb what David called "Culture Mountain."

Ralph was not sure he could afford $12,000 to pay David for six weeks. Ralph was between a rock and a hard place. He had a family to feed and a job that may soon stop feeding them. David said to Ralph, "You have forty-five days, and you need to make a decision."

Chapter 3
Culture Eats Strategy for Breakfast

R alph was caught off guard when David said he wanted to charge him for his help. He didn't know what to do; $12,000 was a lot of money. On the other hand, Ralph had heard from Linda that her uncle charged up to $100,000 for an hour-long speech. After thinking about the amount of money, Ralph reluctantly agreed, but David saw Ralph's hesitance and said, "You know what? It is not worth my time to work with you."

Ralph did not know what to say. David got up to pay and Ralph also stood and said, "It's my treat." David told Ralph that he accepted him paying for breakfast. Then he said, "Please sit down." At this point, Ralph knew some conditions were coming. He had seen this behavior before, not only from David, but also from some of the professional grocery store buyers he had called on for many years.

David told Ralph he would meet with him at different breakfast places and that they would eat for one hour and discuss his upcoming week. David told Ralph that these places were meant to remind Ralph "Culture eats strategy for breakfast," and that he would be responsible for discovering the mind-sets and behaviors he needed to "climb Culture Mountain." David also told Ralph that on any given week, he would decide as a coach if he would continue to work with Ralph or not, and that weekly payment had to be made regardless, and that full payment was due even if David decided to end the agreement with Ralph on any given week. David said, "We pay up weekly. You are not on a forty-five-day performance improvement plan with me. You are on a seven-day plan."

David ordered another cup of coffee and told Ralph that his first session would start right then. Ralph also ordered more coffee. The meaning of "culture eats strategy for breakfast" was now real.

David's true talent was about to be demonstrated live to Ralph, much as Ralph had learned through the school of hard knocks from his previous boss Sam. David asked Ralph to describe the culture at his company. Ralph said that the culture had always been, "Have gun, will travel," and, "What have you done for me lately?"

David said, "I have seen this culture many times, and it is the most common sales culture out there." Ralph was intrigued. He asked David what he meant by that. David next asked Ralph, "Who set this culture?" Ralph told stories about Sam and how he had been trained by him. David explained to Ralph that this was a *transactional* sales culture—one that produced results in the short term but unfortunately led to stress, burnout, high employee turnover, and even physical illnesses and death if not kept under control. Ralph revealed that Sam had, in fact, died from a massive heart attack and that some people at the company had speculated whether it had been related to stress and the high demands of his relentless work ethic. David said he was very sorry to hear this and Ralph started to wonder whether his hero Sam might not have been such a hero after all.

David explained that the right sales culture makes all the difference in getting the results the company wants. Great cultures, he explained, get great results for people *first* and then the company. Poor cultures (like the transactional culture at Ralph's company) lead to worse results because the company puts money first, customers second, and employees third.

At this point, Ralph was confused. Ralph said, "What do you mean about money first versus employees first? Does the order really matter?'

"The order matters a lot," replied David. He explained that most transactional companies think of employees as factors of production who are meant to create results for the companies. This same thing, David said, is true of some countries in which they exploit their people for personal gain.

David ordered water and asked Ralph why his company existed. Ralph said the company existed to produce a profit for the owners, who in this case were also the shareholders. David then asked Ralph, "So, why are *you* there?"

Ralph really had to think about this question. He had never thought about this before. "Well," Ralph said, "I am there to sell and make them money, I guess."

David asked, "Does that inspire you?"

Ralph confided that since Sam had died, he was in fact no longer inspired. In a sense, that was the reason why his performance, morale, and sales had slumped.

David then asked, "Have you ever had sales training?"

"Of course, and lots of it," said Ralph.

"So, what did this training consist of?" asked David. Ralph thought a few seconds and explained that he had been through training on several sales models that had outlined processes and formulas for selling and that the company had set strategies for them to sell more and dominate the market. David asked Ralph to think about whether all these models and strategies had actually helped to change his mind-set and behaviors around selling, and whether they had inspired him to sell more. After thinking about that, Ralph admitted that those efforts had been short-lived; one strategy led to the next, one model was followed by another, and that none of them had ever really been fully implemented.

David then went back to his question: "So, why do you do what you do?"

Ralph's answer that made David smile: "I love selling because I know that the products I sell—snacks—make people happy and unite families around yummy treats."

"So, you sell not to make the company money, or make money for yourself and your family. Your purpose is the people that you sell to? For them to feel even more happiness?" David asked.

"Yes," said Ralph, "that is exactly why I sell. The money is the result of making people happy. It's not just about making money."

David then told the story of Thomas, a commercial fisherman he had worked with who initially saw each fish covered with dollar signs. When he caught fish, he would count the money each one represented. When the business was good, he really liked catching fish. When supplies of fish dwindled, fishing became just a job, though, and not a career, because his main motivation was to catch fish for money and nothing more.

"As I worked with Thomas the fisherman, he began to realize that eating fish was something that also helped people live longer and happier lives," said David. "So, he began to see each fish differently. He saw healthy grandparents playing with their grandchildren because they had eaten his seafood and lived longer healthier lives. Thomas the fisherman became known for helping grandparents everywhere, and that made him really happy. He started to work with joy. I recently saw him become a grandfather and sit down with his own grandchild and eat fish sticks that came from what his fleet of vessels, called grandchildren of the sea, had caught."

The hour was almost over. David asked Ralph what he was going to practice that week. Ralph was excited, and his smile said it all. "I am going to start climbing Culture Mountain by refocusing my priorities. Culture is the most important part of what I do, and having a purpose for what I am selling that is greater than the money I make, as money is the *result* of a higher purpose; it is not *the* higher purpose," replied Ralph. "My purpose is the peak of Culture Mountain, and I always need to live it."

Ralph really enjoyed his first Culture-Eats-Strategy-for-Breakfast meal in Augusta, Georgia, until he remembered that he was supposed to be at a meeting soon with his boss, Mr. Stark. If he didn't hurry, Ralph was going to be late to his first performance improvement plan review. Mr. Stark did not like tardiness, and in this case, Ralph would have to make haste if he was going to get there on time.

Chapter 4
The Cavemen

M r. Stark was quite angry. Ralph had still not shown up, and it was just a couple of minutes before the hour. Mr. Stark thought to himself, "This guy will be late for his first PIP meeting, and that will make this process easier for me."

Just as he was thinking this, Ralph walked into the office with a smile. "Hello, Mr. Stark," he said, knowing he had made it just in time.

"Hello, Ralph. Please sit down," said Mr. Stark. The meeting was full of formalities. Mr. Stark even had a person from Human Resources sit in so the documentation process could continue and someone was there to be a witness.

Ralph kept his composure as he thought about the meeting he had just had with David and the greater purpose of why he was selling. Ralph knew that this higher purpose was going to serve him well as, just for a moment, he placed the financial burden that losing his job would have on the family on the back burner.

Ralph worried a lot about providing for his family. He was the sole wage earner in the household, while Rachel had focused on caring for the house and the children, Becky and Emma (who was now off at college). Rachel had always wanted to work, but that dream had gone away as she had focused on raising their family.

The conversation with Mr. Stark and HR ended: "You will have to show significant sales growth in the next six weeks to get over this PIP. By significant sales growth, I mean a 35 percent increase in your two-month number based on last year."

Ralph thought a second about this. Although he knew it was completely unfair, as his last year numbers during this period had been a record at the company, he also knew that he was not setting the rules now. Ralph left the meeting with a huge weight resting on his shoulders, yet there was something about that higher purpose he had just clarified that was keeping him hopeful. At this point, Ralph also thought about his family and how they were even more important than his higher work purpose. This also gave Ralph more energy to climb Culture Mountain, as David had phrased it.

As Ralph thought of how he was going to tackle the task of growing his numbers by 35 percent year-over-year, he remembered a sales training he had taken in which the instructor had talked about the Pareto Principle, or the 80/20 Rule. The instructor had said, in a nutshell, "80 percent of sales come from 20 percent of the customers," and that focusing on that 20 percent was key to sales success. Ralph had three large grocery store chains that he knew represented almost 80 percent of his business, so he thought they would be the best place to invest his time. He spent the rest of the day calling the accounts and setting appointments for later in the week. He was inspired by making people happy with his products and smiled a lot more than he had in the past few months.

As Ralph sat in a cubicle in the operations group, a plant worker named Ben came by and said, "Hey, Ralph, it is great to see you. And you look happy for the first time in a while! What's the good news?"

Ralph thought to himself that this was the hardest period of his career, yet he was calm and happy. He reflected on how a change in mind-set and perspective had done him good. He thought how powerful this change could be and about how he could keep it going. He knew he would need everything he had to climb Culture Mountain and saw himself cheering when he got to the top.

"Are you OK, Ralph? You know we love you a lot. You always treat us well," said Ben. Ralph really cared about all the front-line workers and always went out of his way to say "Hi" and spend time with everyone at the plant. He had even played on the company soccer team a few seasons and made a lot of friends. Ralph knew that all their hard work contributed to his ability to sell what they worked so hard to produce. Ralph smiled at Ben and got back to work.

Ralph was able to get a meeting on short notice to go see his biggest grocery store chain buyer. He would go to the meeting on Friday and was excited; a good sales call with this client could really help him get to at least 20 percent of the growth he needed to get to the 35 percent that would save his job. As Ralph thought about the upcoming meeting, he also knew that he had some other obligations and paperwork he had not done, as well as expense reports that he knew Mr. Stark wanted to be done before the end of the week.

Ralph spent the rest of the week working on all his backed-up paperwork and expense reports. By the end of the day on Thursday, Ralph entered Mr. Stark's office and handed over all the work, smiling and proud of himself.

"Thanks for doing all this paperwork, Ralph. I really appreciate this hard work, but if you do not make your sales goals, all this will not have been a good use of your time," said Mr. Stark, matter-of-factly. "By the way," he added, "wipe that smile off your face and get to work."

That did it. Ralph's mood changed instantly. Now he was angry with Mr. Stark; his fists involuntarily clenched as if he wanted to go into attack mode. Ralph was so livid that he proceeded to go to the bar on the way home to try to get rid of some of the pent-up stress.

Once at the bar, Ralph found a place next to a couple of rough-looking characters at the end of the bar. Ralph ordered a bourbon on the rocks. As Ralph contemplated his day, he couldn't think of anything but the anger he felt toward Mr. Stark. At one point, Ralph even pounded his fist on the bar. Ralph remembered how he had punched the truck one time when he'd been mad at a customer back when he did route sales for the company. His pinky and middle finger were still crooked from that and actually still caused him pain from time to time. One of the rough-looking men sitting next to Ralph looked at him in a way that made Ralph uncomfortable. Ralph turned to the man and said, "Do you have a problem?"

The man stood up. He was much bigger than Ralph had thought. He seemed like a caveman, complete with a nasty beard full of crumbs from the burger he had just eaten. Ralph was still so angry that he stood up as well. After that, all Ralph remembered was waking up in a strange car.

As it turned out, Ralph's next-door neighbor was also at the bar and had seen the whole incident. Ralph had thrown the first punch, and the next punch was a knock-out blow. Afterward, Ralph's neighbor and friend Fred paid Ralph's bill, apologized to the cavemen, and told the bartender he would take Ralph home.

"Where am I?" Ralph asked as he saw Fred. "What time is it? What are you doing here? What happened?" Ralph tried to collect his thoughts.

He had a small cut on his chin, probably from the ring on the hand of the man who had knocked him out.

Ralph spent some time talking with Fred and then proceeded to go home and face Rachel. When he got home, he explained what had happened. He was not surprised when Rachel did not take it lightly. Instead of consoling Ralph, she called *him* a caveman and said, "Cavemen sleep on couches."

Ralph settled onto the couch for the evening. Even Becky came up and called him a loser. Ralph felt terrible as he struggled to go to sleep. Finally, he got up and went to the kitchen to get some ice for his jaw. He drifted off to sleep with anger still running through his veins. That night, he dreamed about himself and some friends dressed as cavemen fighting a tyrannosaurus rex. Before they were all just about to be eaten, Ralph woke up.

Chapter 5
Failing to Prepare Means Preparing to Fail

Ralph awakened with a locked jaw and the feeling that he was back in a pit of despair. As he moaned on the couch, Rachel came over to him and said, "You men are a bunch of cavemen." She then proceeded to tell Ralph that he'd better get his things in order or she might leave him. Rachel got emotional at times, and Ralph knew when she was serious; she was serious when she said the word "divorce" several times.

Ralph remembered that he had to be at the meeting with his largest customer in just a couple hours. The customer was across town, and it would take a while to get there because there would still be traffic at this time of the morning. Ralph interrupted Rachel and said, "I have a really important sales call today, and I need to prepare." Rachel stopped speaking and Ralph quickly headed to the bathroom to get ready.

Despite his rough night, Ralph felt good when he got out of the shower. He was glad that his face looked normal and the cut on his chin was not all that noticeable, as it was covered by a small second chin he had acquired from gaining some weight recently. Ralph dressed nicely and remembered Sam had always said, "You have to dress for success." Ralph had taken this advice to heart and always ironed all his clothes and made sure to shave and groom properly.

The morning traffic was not as bad as it usually was. Ralph was thinking of what he would say to the client to convince him to load in some extra product so he could make his sales quota. Ralph's relationship with the buyer was OK; he was sure the buyer would help him out.

Lost in his thoughts, Ralph was in such a hurry he simply did not see the stop sign. The police officer was on his tail instantly, and Ralph was immediately scared. As he maneuvered quickly to pull over, however, the police vehicle sped up and passed him. Ralph thought that maybe he had gotten lucky and the police had been called for something else. The police car kept speeding away from him and Ralph let out a sigh of relief. He had cleared that obstacle and now hoped this same luck would help him at the headquarters of the grocery chain.

As Ralph neared the headquarters, he was hoping to find a visitor parking space. He had forgotten to call ahead, so the guard at the gate told him he had to park at the lot across the street. Ralph knew he would need to hustle to get there on time for his appointment. He kept running what he was going to say through his head and couldn't stop thinking about how much he needed this sales call to go well.

As Ralph neared the front desk, he saw Linda sitting in the reception area. Linda was responsible for another segment of the business and was probably there to see another buyer. Ralph checked in and sat next to Linda. Linda was reviewing the preparation she had done for the call. She had brought sales reports, brochures, written questions, and even knew the goals she had for the sales call. Ralph, meanwhile, was busy thinking about what he would say and had even forgotten to bring a pad of paper and pen to take notes. Ralph was empty-handed; Linda was ready for the sales call.

Linda was asked to come in, and Ralph sat there another ten minutes before he got the call to come see the buyer. He saw Linda talking with the buyer in another office, and it looked like from the smiles that the meeting was going well. Ralph was hoping for the same luck in his call. Unfortunately, the buyer Ralph was going to see had already had a rough day. He had just had a salesman refuse to lower his price and walk out on him when Ralph came into his office with a smile on his face.

"What are you smiling about, Ralph?" asked the buyer. Ralph wiped the smile off his face and sat down. Ralph knew this was not a good sign and that he was in trouble from the start. Ralph's anger from the day before, his rough night, problems at home and now a tough buyer overwhelmed him all at once. Ralph knew about the importance of attitude, and unfortunately, he was not prepared for the onslaught of emotion that had just come over him.

For the next few minutes, the buyer reminded Ralph about the last meeting they'd had and how Ralph had come late and unprepared. When he confronted Ralph and asked him what he had done differently this time and whether he had brought the latest projections, knew what the advertising and promotion schedule was, and had a brochure about three new products the buyer had seen in *Snack Food Digest*, Ralph shook his head "no" to each question. In a fit of frustration, the buyer sent Ralph away. Not only did he not want to help him, but he was also going to decrease his purchases by 5 percent.

Ralph left the call defeated. He and Linda met outside and decided to go to lunch. Linda had completed a very successful sales call, and her sales with this account were up by 20 percent.

Ralph talked to Linda about how badly things had gone and commented on how the only bright spot in his life at the moment had been the meeting with her Uncle David.

Linda warned Ralph that Uncle David was really tough with people; he fought to get the very best out of them. She told Ralph that he had fired her and refused to help her when she first asked for his help. She recommended that Ralph prepare for his meeting with David by writing down all the things that had gone well since their first meeting and the points for improvement—*not failures*—that he had to work on.

"If you come to David and start talking about failures, he will quickly end the meeting," confided Linda. "He likes the term 'points of improvement,' because he feels we are all going to fail a lot and he says we should focus on the future, not the past, and that we should talk about what we will do to fix our mistakes the next time around." Linda then said, "Make sure you stress the positives first and how you have changed your mind-set and behaviors when you talk to David. He loves the positives and people who take action. He believes we all know what we should do to be great in sales and what we lack is action."

Ralph was thankful for the conversation with Linda, as he knew that written preparation was not his strength and he really liked to wing it. As Ralph thought about written preparation over the weekend, he was inspired to type up his preparation for David and even to put it into three slides (he remembered Linda saying over dinner that her uncle liked slides). Ralph spent about four hours preparing for his Monday breakfast meeting with David in Charleston, where David was working for the big paper mill. They would meet for breakfast at 8:00 a.m.

As proud as Ralph was of his written preparation for the meeting, he was just as uncomfortable with the situation at home. Rachel and Becky were not talking with him, so he'd thought he would at least get some smiles from his older daughter, Emma, home from college for the weekend. But as it turned out, Emma had just broken up with her boyfriend, and of course Ralph blew the conversation by lecturing her and not listening. Belatedly, Ralph realized he should have prepared himself mentally and emotionally to talk with his family as well as his customers; preparation was not only useful at work. In another period of feeling down, Ralph searched for a half-remembered quote from another training that would help him greatly, both now and in the future. The quote was:

"By failing to prepare, you are preparing to fail." It is often attributed to Benjamin Franklin, but on this night, because he was preparing thoroughly,

Ralph actually went to the Franklin archive to find out where and when he'd written it and was surprised to discover there was no record of Franklin ever having said or written it. Ralph decided he didn't care who originally said it, though; even the act of trying to find the source of the quote proved it to be 100 percent true.

Chapter 6
Talking Is Not Your Friend

As part of his preparation, Ralph again departed very early in the morning and arrived a little before the appointed time at the restaurant, Acme Lowcountry Kitchen in Isle of Palms, where David had directed him in a calendar invitation. Ralph had prepared what he wanted to say to David and had put it in writing, awakening at 5:30 a.m. so he could gather his thoughts and be there ahead of time. A few minutes before 8:00 a.m., David walked up to the restaurant as it was about to open, and saw Ralph already there. Ralph said "Hi," as David stared at Ralph. Ralph softened his smile, and finally, David smiled back.

"So, how are you doing, Ralph? What has gone well this week?" asked David.

Ralph was caught off guard as all he could think of was what had gone wrong that week. Ralph was quiet for a few seconds to gather his thoughts and then said, "I worked for the greater purpose of making people happy. I started the week with this thought, and it carried me through the week on a positive note: 'The purpose really matters.'"

"Why is the purpose so important to you?" asked David.

"It is the driving force of a person or a company," said Ralph. "Purpose is what should be our compass and focal point. It is what keeps us pointed in the right direction and should drive us to do the right thing. It is the lighthouse to guide us forward."

"That's a great answer," said David. "So, how are you living this purpose in your personal and professional life?"

"Well, not so well," said Ralph while looking down and feeling sorry for himself. Ralph knew he should keep it positive; he had started that way but then quickly went to the negative with David. Ralph could tell that David was already starting to get upset. He was scowling at Ralph because the pity party had already started.

"Listen, Ralph," said David, "I talked with Linda, and she briefed me on the talk she had with you. As she said, I like to talk about the future and not explore the past, so before you frustrate me, tell me what you learned this week that will help you do better."

"I learned that I am a caveman at heart, and that I have to control my emotions, how I act, and what I say," said Ralph. David started to nod, and Ralph continued. "I also learned that no matter how much someone pushes my buttons, I am always in control of how I act and need to consciously regulate this. I also learned that lack of preparation had been haunting me my whole life, and that I could have done much better in life, school, home, and every place else if I had prepared myself mentally, emotionally, and in writing before getting into situations in which I failed due to lack of written preparation."

David (who only smiled when something was really great) was smiling. "On top of what you learned—and more importantly Ralph—how will you change your mind-set and behaviors to correct your mistakes and get on a better path?" asked David.

"I am going to go to my sales calls prepared in writing and even prepare my attitude ahead of time before I face situations at work and at home," said Ralph. "I will also adopt a more positive attitude and smile, always expecting the best instead of thinking of the worst-case scenario. I will not provoke fights, either physical or emotional, and will watch what I say and how I act to create peace versus war. I will not complain about the hills so I can reach the top of the mountain—Culture Mountain."

"Those are really great attitudes and behaviors to work on, Ralph, and I like how you said you would do them, rather than *try* or *think* you would do them. Great job," said David. "Now that we have determined that happiness is at the peak of Culture Mountain, let's put on our climbing shoes and tackle that mountain. We will reach three summits in the next weeks, and it will take hard work, both physically and mentally, for you to get there. Are you ready, Ralph?"

Ralph nodded a yes and leaned forward even more.

At this point, the server came over and asked for their order. Ralph ordered the McClellanville which comes with sauteed shrimp, sauteed kale and poached eggs on an english muffin with hollandaise. David ordered grits with cheese. They both had coffee.

"Each of the steps up Culture Mountain will be a value that you have to live, with specific behaviors you have to consciously practice over time until they become habits," said David. "The first stop on the climb will be to live the value of *constant curiosity* as a major sales and even a leadership mind-set. What are some behaviors you have to engage in to be curious?"

Ralph thought about his answer for a moment. Then he said, "To be constantly curious seems annoying to me David. It seems pushy."

David frowned and stayed quiet.

"On the other hand," said Ralph, "you have to ask a lot of questions and really listen if you want to be constantly curious, and that may mean that instead of talking, you take an interest in other people. And maybe if you do, they will also take an interest in you."

"That's right," said David, "and here are a few tips for making sure you ask the right types of questions. You will want to write these down." Ralph dutifully started writing.

1. Ask open versus closed questions. Open questions have more than one right answer and start with the words *who*, *what*, *where*, *when*, *why* and *how*. If your questions don't start with these words, you are asking closed questions (which adults usually ask, because they think they know everything) versus open questions, which children ask (because they want to learn everything).

2. Ask a variety of *why* and *how* questions so that you can figure out the reasoning behind a person's thinking. Don't go right into the specific details of *who*, *what,* and *where*.

"I'm warning you, Ralph," David continued, "this will be really difficult, and you will have to practice this purposefully, as your subconscious and previous habits will fight against you. How have you seen me using questions in my meetings with you?"

"I see that you ask me a variety of open and closed questions and take an interest in me," Ralph replied. He reflected that he had a lot to work on between focusing on his purpose, preparing in writing, and asking open questions. Ralph was excited to see that these behaviors were going to help him.

The rest of the meeting, Ralph showed David his written preparation and slides. David seemed to love that Ralph was starting to get it, but said he was worried that with only several weeks left, Ralph was going to have to drink from a firehose, absorb the water and make it part of his way of life.

On the way back to Columbia, Ralph was able to practice open questions as he talked with clients over the speakerphone to set appointments. He also checked in with Mr. Stark as he was supposed to; some of his questions were so good he thought even Mr. Stark was surprised.

Ralph was so excited from his meeting that he was not paying attention to his speed. The flashing lights eventually came, and Ralph did not practice constant curiosity with the officer, instead talking so much that he seemed to annoy the dutiful representative of the law. At the end of their roadside visit, the officer ended up giving

Ralph a ticket *and* points. Ralph was once again overwhelmed and thought, "I talk too much; this is the plight of the salesperson." Ralph also realized he would be late now to his next sales call. "When it rains, it pours bad luck," thought Ralph.

Chapter 7
What Did You Say?

Ralph spent the whole next week focusing on the purpose of why he was selling, preparing in writing for his sales meetings, and focusing on being more curious and asking open questions that started with the words *who*, *what*, *where*, *when*, *why* and *how*. He also asked more *why* questions and especially enjoyed asking, "Why is that important for you?" He also began questions with, "I am just curious, why..." That seemed to also really help.

Throughout the week, Ralph reflected that, instead of talking and acting like a caveman, he was actually becoming more of a human being and caring more about people. He realized that he had never uncovered so many needs in his life as he was now and that sales were actually becoming more about the buyer than it was about him.

Ralph was also more conscious of his caveman behaviors with Rachel and Becky, and that was leading them to have much better relationships at home. Ralph's wife had even said, "I find you much more attractive this week than I have for a while." Becky had actually taken the time to sit down and talk with Ralph for longer than five minutes. This had been a great week at home as well as work.

Ralph was seeing for himself that the value of constantly being curious was something that top salespeople (including himself in the past) had in spades, and it was the most important thing he could be doing with clients—actually, where he should spend 80 percent of his time. As a result, Ralph took the time to actually go to the stores of his three top clients. He asked the route salesperson for his company and the clerks and store managers what they wanted and why certain promotions and products sold more than others. Ralph also asked people what they thought was going well in the store and where his company could improve. Ralph then compiled all that information, sales reports, and then went and spoke with people in marketing at his company for the first time in quite a while.

With all the research and preparation Ralph had done, he went to see his second-largest account at the end of the week. Through preparation, open questions, and hard work, Ralph was able to get the buyer to increase his orders by 15 percent. Also, Ralph had found in his visits to the stores that some space in the stores that his company had been paying for was actually being taken up by a competitor's products. Ralph brought this to the attention of the buyer and was able to pass the information along to the route salespeople so they could stock the extra space. Ralph also communicated this to Mr. Stark, who congratulated Ralph on the due diligence and extra effort he had put into bringing the issue to light. Mr. Stark let him know this was going to benefit the company, as the same competitor was taking advantage of the same arrangement in other grocery store chains.

Ralph's great efforts for the week did not, unfortunately, compensate for his mistake with his largest customer the week before. Although his sales were up by 3 percent overall, he still had a long way to go to get to the 35 percent year-over-year increase that would save his job.

Ralph again spent the weekend preparing for his meeting with David. He put his slides together, remembering David telling him to keep it to three slides and to use the four-by-four rule. David had spent some time explaining to Ralph that less was more and that there was brilliance in simplicity. David had explained to Ralph that in slides, he should include no more than four points per slide and no more than four words per point: hence, the four-by-four rule. David had also advised to Ralph that he should include appropriate pictures because, as the old saying goes, they are worth a thousand words.

Ralph also prepared the questions he wanted to ask David when he saw him that week. Some of the questions Ralph wrote down were:

- Why are salespeople not as respected as they should be?

- How can we sell more?

- What are the qualities of a great salesperson?

Ralph was getting into the groove of his pre-dawn drives to breakfast. He arrived at the Biscuit Head breakfast place in Greenville, South Carolina at 7:00 a.m. when they opened, knowing that David would not be able to be there until 7:15. Ralph liked the atmosphere at this breakfast place and had read reviews in advance, so he knew they were famous for having a jam bar for their biscuits. Ralph ordered some coffee and eyed the menu. The moment he saw a Mimosa Fried Chicken Biscuit, he decided that was what he would order. As David was pretty fit, Ralph knew that at some point he would probably point out he should watch himself in this area and start eating better. Ralph had been an athlete growing up but had let his physical condition slip a bit as he concentrated on his family and career.

Ralph was so excited to see David that he could hardly contain himself. His successes putting into practice what David had suggested and his re-found curiosity made him eager to ask David the questions that he had prepared. Ralph was also a bit nervous; he was paying David $2,000 each time they met, and he was taking this out of household savings. He did not want to get fired and owe David the money for all these sessions; at the same time, he could barely afford to pay David. Ralph had hoped that David wouldn't charge him, but then remembered that if you give away something for free, people frequently do not take it seriously. On further reflection, Ralph decided that paying the money was worth it. He knew it helped hold him accountable. It did hurt, however, to recall he had not yet told Rachel about the money.

Ralph also knew that he was in the start of his third week on the performance improvement plan (PIP) and that he did not have a lot of time left to reach the sales growth target that he needed to stay at the company. Since Ralph had been at the company a long time and the benefits were good, he was also afraid that he would lose it all, and that it would take time to find another position.

David walked into the restaurant with the same reserve as always. This time, Ralph imitated his same tone and body language. He had found that when he did this with people (at least within reason), it helped to set the meeting on an even footing and even build rapport and respect. Ralph was feeling good. He was going to have a great meeting.

David started by ordering some coffee and looking at the menu. "What has gone well for you this week?" David asked Ralph.

Ralph went on for eight minutes telling David what he had done during the week and how well his sales endeavors had gone. David listened attentively—until he didn't. David then got up and left the restaurant.

He did not return.

Ralph sat there alone for a while and ordered his biscuit. Slowly, dismay dawned. He could not believe that David had just walked out on him without saying anything. Ralph was about to get really angry when he remembered what had happened at the bar. The caveman inside him had to contain itself.

Ralph dialed David several times and got his voicemail. Ralph thought about all the preparation he had done, all the work he had put in, only to have been left stranded. Ralph then remembered all that David had taught him and thought maybe there was a lesson to be learned from the morning's events.

As Ralph drove back to Columbia, he knew he had his weekly meeting with Mr. Stark and had also scheduled a meeting with his third-largest account, both in the afternoon.

"Are you even listening to me?" asked Mr. Stark. Ralph continued to interrupt as he talked about all the wonderful things he had accomplished the week before. "I know why you have trouble, Ralph," continued Mr. Stark. Before he could get out another word, Ralph continued to steamroll through conversation. Mr. Stark finally ended the meeting by saying, "You are still way behind. You don't seem to be learning, and you have only a little more than three weeks left."

Ralph had prepared questions for his meeting with Mr. Stark, and even though he asked the questions, he had proceeded to answer them himself. Ralph then finally got through to David, who told him he was fired as a client. Ralph asked questions, and David merely answered calmly that he had to go and to please send a check for the balance of the rest of the sessions.

At this point, Ralph was more than upset. He knew that he had blown it, but did not realize what he had done wrong.

The sales call that afternoon went OK. Ralph left with a 10 percent increase in orders, even though he interrupted the buyer several times and could have probably gotten more if he had just stayed quiet.

Ralph arrived home and proceeded to go down to his man cave, where he was hoping to relax in peace and quiet after a long, tough day. Rachel then came downstairs and proceeded to ask about his day. Ralph talked and talked, hoping that Rachel could understand and help him solve the issues. Rachel then started talking about her own issues and could tell Ralph was getting annoyed.

Ralph thought to himself, "Not only did she not help me with my issues; now she is filling my head with *her* issues that I really could not care less about." As Ralph worked to appear as if he was listening, he thought about how much money he had wasted on David and how annoying Rachel's monologue was. Ralph knew he was about to see the wrath of Rachel as he could see the veins in her neck begin to stand out and venom begin to show on her red face.

"You do not listen, and worst of all, you do not care," said Rachel. Ralph asked Rachel to go away. She rapidly obliged.

Ralph then called his friend Chip, who he knew would listen to him and also offer some solutions. As Ralph talked to Chip, Rachel came back down and interrupted the conversation to say that she was contacting an attorney in the morning to start divorce proceedings. Ralph made matters much worse when he said, "What did you just say?"

Ralph's wife stormed out.

Ralph said goodbye to Chip and went to watch the football game and go to sleep on the couch.

Chapter 8
You Have Objections?

R alph woke up predawn the next morning, checked his email, and discovered more pain and suffering. Ralph's top account had not received their promotional shipment and Ralph had to run into the plant to see what was going on. While at the plant, Ralph overheard someone call him "loudmouth Ralph."

Ralph was able to get the missing shipment expedited and now had a chance to think about what the person had said in the hallway a few minutes earlier. Ralph finally understood why David had walked out on him and why his previous day had gone so poorly. Ralph said to himself, "I need to shut up and listen."

As soon as Ralph saw the light, he called and left a voicemail for David. Ralph apologized to David and said he had learned his lesson "through the school of hard knocks." Ralph sounded sincere and realized that he needed David's help if he was going to make it in a good way, not only in business but also in life.

David called Ralph back later and offered to meet him in Columbia, South Carolina, as he had a business meeting there. He would meet him for a late breakfast at The Gourmet Shop Café in Five Points. Ralph knew the place well. It had been a staple of great food in Columbia since the 1970s. Ralph made sure to listen carefully to David and even let him hang up the phone before Ralph hung up. Ralph was hoping the meeting would go well and that he would get a chance to learn something else that could help him.

Next, Ralph called his friend Chip back, and the two had a great conversation. Chip said that he knew Ralph was a loudmouth and that even though he had told Ralph to watch that in the past, he knew it would take a hard lesson for Ralph to learn. Ralph, Chip said, was stubborn and not always willing to listen to advice, but Chip was starting to see the changes in his friend and even complimented Ralph on listening and asking open questions as they were on the phone together.

Ralph arrived at the Café and got a table outside. As soon as David arrived, Ralph was very courteous. He asked David questions and listened.

David then asked Ralph, "Why should I keep working with you, Ralph? You talk too much, and I am not sure if you are going to make it." David waited for Ralph to speak; he seemed to be waiting for Ralph to blow this opportunity.

Ralph had been taught in a sales program to handle objections, however, and surprised David by saying, "I hear that you said 'why should I keep working with you,' that I talk too much, and that you are not sure I will make it,'" Ralph said. Ralph then asked David, "Then why are you here?"

David smiled and congratulated Ralph by saying, "You have obviously been trained well to handle objections, haven't you Ralph? You were silent and listened to my objection. You then repeated my exact words, and then you asked me a question to follow up, which in this case did not escalate the objection. I am proud of you, Ralph, and that you are preparing in writing, asking open questions, and also listening. All these habits show curiosity, which is the value we talked about first. These behaviors also show the second important value, which is *accountability*. If you have curiosity and accountability with a purpose other than money, you are two-thirds of the way to being a great salesperson, not to mention a leader."

Ralph was gratified to hear that he was becoming more conscious of his behaviors and that this was helping him to purposely reap better outcomes. He shared this insight and got David to smile again. David needed Ralph to learn these things on his own; he was combining the positive reinforcement of smiles and praise with "tough love" to make sure Ralph was held accountable and remained curious of the conscious values he was putting into practice. In this way, they would eventually become habits.

"Accountability is one of the things I have lacked recently," Ralph confessed. "I used to keep learning and never took 'No' for an answer when I first started selling. I have lost that accountability—to hold myself responsible, to continue to keep trying and going from failure to failure more quickly so I can be a success. I need to regain that will to win, to hold myself accountable for the things I do well and to do better on things I can improve, like listening."

"I do not think you can just regain accountability," David whispered to Ralph.

Ralph recognized another objection and without blinking an eye, stayed silent to ensure he had listened thoroughly. Hearing no further input, he said, "So, David, I heard you say that you do not think I can just regain accountability." Ralph then asked, "How accountable have I been listening to your objections and handling them consciously?"

David smiled again and said, "Bravo Ralph. You are doing things on purpose and taking accountability for your actions and words. Awesome."

David and Ralph continued to exchange ideas about how to get Ralph to make his ambitious sales target in the very few weeks he had left. At the end of the meeting, Ralph paid David and said, "Thank you."

Ralph walked out feeling like a winner for the first time in a long while. He felt more competitive, more accountable, and more alive than he had in some time. He realized that besides the paycheck he was earning, he really liked growing as a person and appreciated that David was empowering him to change himself. Ralph knew that he had a little less than three weeks left to make the goal. Now he was energized to tackle the big obstacle: getting his largest client to increase their orders so he could get over the hump preventing him from continuing his career at the company and blocking the chance to put more wins on the Wall of Fame at the plant.

Ralph spent the rest of the day visiting the stores of his largest account and talking with people at the store level to understand their needs even better. He also listened and handled objections from the sales route drivers for his company.

When Ralph came home, he saw that Rachel and Becky had some of their suitcases by the door. When Ralph called out to them, Rachel came over and said, "We are going to my mom's house so you can figure out if you want a family or not."

Ralph was devastated by this news and broke down crying.

Chapter 9
How Human Are You?

Ralph fell asleep on the couch, drinking beer, crying, and watching ESPN. When he awakened early the following morning, he realized the home crisis had distracted him from preparing for his big meeting with his top customer.

He quickly got ready, prepared a goal for the meeting, and thought through the open questions he wanted to ask in writing. He prepared for the objections he would receive with counter-questions he could ask to keep the dialogue going and get the buyer closer to a close on the sale. He was also prepared to listen and keep a positive attitude, liking the buyer no matter what. He reminded himself of the two values—being curious and accountable—then left for the meeting.

Ralph arrived at the buyer's office with about ten minutes to spare. He spent the ten minutes preparing his materials and visualizing the outcome he wanted. He also saw the monthly newsletter the grocery store put out on a side table. Since he only had a couple minutes left, instead of reading the newsletter, he decided to keep preparing his materials.

Ralph was escorted in by one of the assistants, who took him to see a person he did not recognize. It turned out the buyer Ralph had seen for years had been promoted. The assistant saw the surprised look on Ralph's face and said, "Did you not know that Chuck had been promoted? It was in the newsletter and everything."

Ralph was polite and instantly knew that all the preparation he had done was for the wrong buyer. He would have to get to know this buyer extremely quickly. Time was running out. Ralph met the new buyer, Horace, and recognized that he was a very nice person, extremely tall, and looked as if he may have played football in the past. Ralph saw that Horace liked to talk and even went as far as talking about his family and how long he had lived in Columbia, South Carolina. Ralph knew he was there to sell and went straight to business. He had all the facts and figures for Horace. He asked great questions and handled some objections well.

At the end of the meeting, Ralph asked Horace for the order, which was larger than usual. Horace said that he would place the normal order and thanked Ralph for coming in. Ralph was disappointed that he had not gotten the larger order. With only two-and-a-half weeks left in his PIP, he knew he was doomed to fail without more sales in this account.

Ralph thought for a while and decided to call David and talk about his experience. David answered Ralph's call. Ralph explained what had happened with the buyer. David explained to Ralph that the last value he would talk further with him about the next week was people skills and that a great part of people skills was the ability to read people quickly and mirror their behavior. On a basic level, David explained to Ralph that people like to be treated the way they are, and that to create a connection, it was important to connect with a person as they want to be connected with. David went on to tell Ralph that the new buyer was a people person and wanted to engage on a personal level before doing business. Ralph explained that in his urgency to be accountable, he had forgotten to be human.

David suggested Ralph quickly call the buyer back and see if he could meet him for coffee. Ralph said that this would probably not work, as buyers were not usually very personable and that the previous buyer would have never met him for coffee. David insisted that Ralph try to do something with the buyer outside of work or even invite him to a store with a Starbucks in it so they could tour the displays of snacks. That way Ralph could have coffee with him at the store without buying him a coffee—he could keep everything very professional.

Ralph took David's advice and invited Horace to meet at one of the larger stores that Friday morning. As Ralph took Horace through the displays, he asked Horace questions about him, his past experiences, and from what he saw, what he thought they were doing well and what they could improve. As Ralph got more human with Horace, Horace got happier with Ralph. Soon they were sitting having coffee and talking about personal things for an hour. Horace explained to Ralph that his company's products were very important for him; the profit margins were excellent, and the snacks carried a lot of weight with customers due to extensive advertising. They talked about college football and connected on the basis that both were big South Carolina Gamecock fans. By the end of their meeting, Ralph had invited Horace to come to a tailgate spot that he shared with friends he had gone to college with.

That weekend, Ralph met Horace at the tailgate. They ate and drank some beers together and even threw the football around with the kids. Horace had to leave to go meet some other friends and said to Ralph, "Come by and see me next Wednesday. I have a great idea for your products."

Ralph prepared to go meet David again, and this time they had arranged to meet in Savannah. David did a lot of work for paper, packaging, and wood products companies. This week, he was in Savannah talking with a few of those companies. It would represent most of the day on the road, but Ralph was *all in*. He drove down the night before and got a good night's sleep in a comfortable but affordable motel so he'd be alert and prepared first thing in the morning.

David met Ralph at Henry's in Savannah at 6:30 a.m. Both ordered Eggs Benedict Florentine style, with spinach and mushrooms. This was a longer meeting than the others; David and Ralph talked about the third value of great salespeople, which was the ability to employ great people skills. They talked about personality styles and how, on a basic level, people were either people- or task-oriented, and either introverts or extroverts. The people that were more task-oriented and extroverts David called "red style."

"These people like communication that is short, and are results-oriented, and care mostly about getting things done," said David. "There is another group of people who lead more with a people orientation and are extroverted. This is the yellow team. Horace is one of these people. They like leading with people and enjoy being social and talking about personal things. These people genuinely value other people who involve them and take an interest in them and their ideas and visions."

Others, David said, led with what David called green energy, which was also people-oriented individuals who are more introverted. The people who lead with this style care about others and like stability. They need for people to show them they care. The last color David talked about was the blue group, whom he said were more task-oriented introverts, and the thing they like the most is to be informed and to get as many details as possible. Almost every person, David said, has every color in their personality. Most lead with one color, though, and by meeting and mirroring them, it is possible to create better rapport.

David explained that emotional intelligence is about knowing about people's feelings. He explained that we all have emotional bank accounts with people and that we either add to them when we meet them where they are or withdraw from them when we treat them as they do not want to be treated. We either have positive or negative emotional bank accounts with others. When you have a high positive bank account balance, people are more likely to want to buy from you. Since Ralph had met Horace where he liked to be met at the store and the tailgate, he and Horace had added to each other's emotional bank accounts. David also made the analogy that when you get an incoming cell phone call and you recognize a name, you may immediately want to pick it up (a high emotional bank account) or not answer it at all (a negative emotional bank account).

Ralph ended the meeting with David and headed back to Columbia where he had scheduled meetings with all his customers in the next two weeks. He was hoping to hear from Rachel. He called her on the way, but she continued not to return his calls. Ralph was getting worried that his marriage would end. This lack of communication did not help. He knew Rachel was upset. Ralph thought of going out to drink later on but knew he needed to keep his job and save his marriage. Those should be his top priorities.

Although Ralph had the best of intentions at the end of the day, he still went to the bar.

Chapter 10
Why Is Silence a Virtue?

Ralph met Chip at Dr. Rocco's in Five Points in Columbia, South Carolina, and they both had a shot of tequila with the two owners, who were both named Mark. Ralph talked about how he had been talking to David the consultant and both of the Marks remembered having met David and even playing golf with him out at Wildewood Golf Club. One of the Marks was such a great character and person that he was often referred to as "The Mayor of Five Points." You could tell both Marks got along quite well and had lots of fun.

Fortunately for Ralph, he decided to do the smart thing and quit while he was ahead. He headed home to get a good night's sleep before his sales calls the rest of the week. He knew that this week, he needed to close sales or he would be in big trouble. The following week was his last week on the PIP.

Ralph's weekly meetings with Mr. Stark had been going better. He had even identified that he led with a blue color and that's why he liked so much detail in his reports. Ralph, on the other hand, now recognized that he led with the red color personality; that sometimes made him more impatient than he should be.

Ralph had a meeting with his second-largest client, and it went well until it came time to close the business. Ralph was putting into practice all he had learned from David and things were going much better. The only issue now was that when Ralph was about to close the sale and get another increase in orders, he tried to oversell.

He got too ambitious. The buyer said he would have to think about it until next week. Ralph knew that not being quiet was a weakness of his, and this had come out to haunt him yet again. Ralph really needed every sale he could get.

On Wednesday, Ralph met with Horace, and to Ralph's surprise, Horace had given Ralph's company an extra 20 percent of space. When he had looked over the numbers and seen how well the products were doing, Horace could justify giving Ralph's company's products more space. It also did not hurt that Ralph had made an emotional connection with Horace, which would ultimately lead to friendship outside of work.

Ralph had finally heard from Rachel; she told him that she was working with a therapist on being more forthcoming about expressing her needs and was also uncovering childhood issues, which she was working on as well. She did not let Ralph off the hook, though. She said she was not happy in the marriage as it currently stood, and that Ralph had to begin working on his issues as she worked on hers, or it would not survive.

Ralph was somewhat relieved by talking with Rachel. He was also able to talk with both his daughters, Becky and Emma, to clear the air regarding the relationship difficulties between him and their mom. Ralph and Rachel really loved their daughters and were very proud of them; the girls, likewise, both appreciated their mom and dad a lot, although as teenagers, it would sometimes not show up in their behavior.

Ralph's meetings with all his clients went well. It looked as though Ralph would save his job—until Ralph got a call from his second-largest client. Ralph's attempt to oversell the client had turned into a no-order decision. This hit Ralph hard. Just as he was finally seeing the light, his over-talking had backfired on him once again.

The next meeting with David would be in Atlanta. David scheduled the meeting with Ralph at a place called Callie's Hot Little Biscuit in Virginia Highlands. The previous breakfast meeting had gone well with Ralph fresh and rested, and so he made good use of another clean, affordable motel to get to the city ahead of time and to get a good night's sleep before heading to the restaurant. When Ralph arrived, he could tell it was a popular spot as he waited fifteen minutes in line to get a seat. David met him in the line, and they talked about the last week. David asked Ralph what had gone well that week and what he needed to improve. Ralph was humble as he talked about the success with Horace and also about losing the sale with his second-largest client because he oversold at the end of the sale.

"Congratulations, Ralph, on building a relationship with Horace in a short amount of time and winning the right to get the sales with him," said David. "Also, congratulations on all your sales calls and the fact you practiced the three values of curiosity, accountability, and people skills," continued David. "What do you feel you can improve with the loss of the sales to your second largest account?"

Ralph took some time to think and also have a piece of his fried chicken biscuit he had convinced David to split with him. "I felt I needed to stop selling," said Ralph.

"Think about who is nervous when you go to close a sale," David offered.

"The customer is nervous because they are spending a lot of money," Ralph answered.

Ralph thought a bit more, and David stayed quiet. As a matter of fact David was quiet for a while. "Me, as the salesperson—I am also nervous because in this case, my job depends on this sale," said Ralph. David remained quiet for what seemed like three minutes and Ralph started to eat his breakfast and drink his coffee. "I should have stayed quiet," said Ralph, finally. "That shows confidence and also calms the other person in a tough position."

Ralph was excited. He had discovered yet another key sales behavior that was critically important in selling or helping another person buy. Ralph was finally getting what David had spent weeks allowing him to discover through wins and losses. Ralph was delighted that he had met David. When he realized that his last breakfast with David would be the next week, he got melancholy, but the sadness went away as he handed the $2,000 check to David.

Ralph had scheduled his meeting with Mr. Stark in the afternoon so he had time to get back to Columbia from Atlanta. Ralph had been smart and prepared a report in writing to give to Mr. Stark, as he had the week before. He could tell Mr. Stark had been happy with that report; Mr. Stark's personality was attuned to the preparation and details Ralph had put into it and he was even showing this report to others as an example of what everybody should be turning in.

"So, Ralph," Mr. Stark said as he arrived, "I thought you were going to make it—until I just got a credit we issued to your largest account that did not get taken away from your sales quota last quarter. And I see you did not get the order from your second largest account. I appreciate your efforts and do not want to burst your bubble, but I do not think you are going to make it."

Ralph handled the moment using everything he had learned with David. He stayed quiet for a minute-and-a-half. Finally, Mr. Stark said, "Or maybe you *will* make it." Ralph smiled humbly and left the office.

Just as Ralph was getting his head around how he was going to make up the sales, he got a phone call. The caller ID said it was from a law firm. Ralph's stomach fell and he went totally pale.

Chapter 11

There's Value in the Values

The call from the attorney was actually a cold-call from a lawyer named Jeff, who asked Ralph about his estate plan and will.

Ralph was so relieved it was not a divorce attorney, he actually listened to Jeff and heard that Jeff was using the three values of great salespeople: curiosity, accountability, and great people skills. Ralph asked Jeff if they could meet in a few weeks, and they settled on that.

Ralph had his last meeting with David in Charlotte, North Carolina this time.

Ralph met David on a Sunday this time. He only had a week to get to his sales target, and his meeting with Mr. Stark was early on Monday morning. Ralph met David at Tupelo Honey in Charlotte, where they split some biscuits with honey and blueberry jam and a Wicked Chicken Biscuit. David reviewed their sessions and the important lessons with Ralph:

- The three *values* of great salespeople and how it was important to keep the CAP values (curiosity, accountability, and people skills) front and center

- The adjoining *behaviors* of great salespeople: written preparation, open questions prepared in advance, attentive listening, handling objections, always building the relationship according to the personality, and silence

David emphasized these were important attitudes and habits to keep practicing. David also explained that as Ralph had discovered these values and behaviors through successes and failures, he should continue to use his brain and heart to lead him to further hone these values with best-practice behaviors and that he would continue to discover how he could tie these behaviors to the three values. David called this culture-driven selling and said if Ralph continued to live these values and behaviors, they would be with him the rest of his life and make him extremely successful.

David also asked Ralph a lot of questions about who usually were the best salespeople and what it was about their values, attitudes, and behaviors that made them so good.

"The best salespeople are curious, accountable, and have the people skills to make calls on everyone and know that the more they get 'no' as the answer, the more success they will have," said Ralph. "The best home-run hitters in baseball also have the most strike-outs. They also know that curiosity keeps them willing to discover hidden needs that people have that make it easier for them to buy. They ask a lot of questions and listen actively, so they get the customer to convince themselves and see the benefits of buying products and services. The best salespeople show accountability and prepare what they want to ask in writing, anticipate what objections they will get and how to deal with them, know who they should call on with the 80/20 rule in mind, and have the discipline to stay quiet when needed. They also have the people skills to build relationships and meet people where they are, without judging, knowing that if they work with each person as they like to be worked with, both will succeed."

The meeting with David went really well. The two agreed to stay in touch. David emphasized to Ralph that there is always value in having values and that he would not only keep his job, but he would also go on to do great things at the company.

Ralph returned to Columbia and prepared for his meeting the next day with Mr. Stark.

The meeting with Mr. Stark started with the boss telling Ralph that he was not going to make it. Ralph handled the objection, asked great questions, offered plenty of information in the style he liked and showed great poise by remaining quiet when needed. Mr. Stark ended the meeting by letting Ralph know the numbers were not there yet and that he only had one week left to get them up to keep his job.

When Ralph left the meeting, he got a call from Rachel. She said she wanted to go to relationship counseling with Ralph and told him that she had found a great therapist. Ralph knew it was now or never. He explained his work situation and even told her about the money he had paid David for his help. She was initially angry that he had not told her about the money, but then told Ralph that she thought it was a good investment if it ended up saving his job. They had a good conversation, and Ralph agreed to go to the counseling once he got through the week.

Ralph was still considerably behind his target and went to talk with Horace. Horace was happy to help Ralph as long as Ralph was willing to get his people to build displays and do a contest at every store to give away a college-football-themed grill.

Ralph went to talk with Mr. Stark, who rejected the contest idea and told Ralph that he could not just create a contest to save his job. Ralph showed Mr. Stark the numbers and was persistent in a polite way, but Mr. Stark refused to give approval until he'd had more time to review the proposal.

Next, Ralph went to his other customers to make the last push and found that there was a little hope in his second-largest customer—the one he thought was least likely to help him.

With only one day left to make his quota, Ralph had nearly lost hope that he would make it. He decided to go to Five Points to get a quick beer with his friend Chip. As he was talking with one of the Marks, Ralph mentioned his perilous situation. Mark said to Ralph that the buyer at his second-largest client was his cousin and that he would be happy to call him to get his help. Mark made the call. The buyer called Ralph and agreed to put in some special displays if Ralph promised his people would adequately merchandise them. Ralph asked him if he could cut the purchase order on Friday; the buyer said that he would.

The next day, Ralph woke up happy knowing that he was going to (just barely) save his job. His day turned much worse, though, as he got a call from his second-largest client; he could not get the purchase order done until Monday. Ralph called Mr. Stark, told him about the purchase order, and asked if he would help him. The answer was no. Mr. Stark then said he had to go to talk with a customer.

Ralph was angry, disappointed, and did not know what to do. He called Horace and was not able to reach him; he was on the other line. Ralph had no choice; he called Rachel and told her the bad news. She took it as well as could be expected, which was not all that well.

Ralph went to see a couple customers to see if a miracle would happen as he thought about the values he had been practicing and how long he had come in the last few weeks. He thought about having to find another job and save his marriage. He got overwhelmed.

Then he got a call from Mr. Stark, and he was sure that it would be bad news. There was no value in the values when you do not have a job and family, he thought.

Chapter 12
Ralph's New Life

Ralph's call with Mr. Stark did not go well. It went *really* well. Mr. Stark had, in fact, authorized the promotional contest with Horace, who had called him directly and said he wanted the promotion for the whole grocery store chain, not just the region that Ralph covered. This meant that not only had Ralph made his number—*all* the salespeople in the region had *also* made their number. *For the next six months.*

Mr. Stark congratulated Ralph on all this hard work and let him know that his job was secure if he kept up the great work. Ralph's phone also started blowing up with calls from all the people in his division, thanking him for the largest sale in the history of the chain. Horace had called all the other buyers for the country and made the order so large that Mr. Stark had ordered college football grills as a promotional giveaway for the whole country.

Ralph was so excited about the news, he quickly shared it with Rachel and with David. Rachel was really excited for Ralph. She understood his pain and suffering about the job and the family and the large burden on him to provide for the family. Ralph also understood all the work Rachel had done raising their children and was thankful to her for that. David said he had great news for Ralph also, as he said a gift was coming for Ralph via overnight delivery, arriving the next day.

The following morning, Ralph received a check for $12,000 from David and a $120 gift certificate for the Gourmet Shop in Atlanta with a personal note from David congratulating him on overcoming his PIP and his start in culture-driven selling. "Culture really does eat strategy for breakfast, so enjoy your breakfast with the family at the Gourmet Shop in Columbia." David also wrote that he hoped his experience would help the company embrace culture over process-driven programs.

Ralph immediately called David and thanked him for all he had done and for the wonderful, completely unexpected present. Ralph promised David he would continue the culture-driven selling and that culture would be his main focus in the future.

Ralph stuck with his commitment to go see the counselor with Rachel, and eventually Emma and Becky also joined for a couple of whole-family sessions. They all benefited from the help of Luis the psychologist, who asked the whole family to practice the value of compassion for each other. This value became the pinnacle of the values for

Ralph's family, and they became a culture-driven home, as well.

Compassion helped Ralph become not only one of the best husbands and dads, but also helped Ralph and the people around him to be truly happy. Compassion was a value that went with the values of curiosity, accountability, and people skills; Ralph called these the CCAPS that pointed him in the right direction for the rest of his life.

Ralph continued to do well in sales at the snack foods company. After several years, eventually, he was promoted to President and CEO. For supporting him in his own way when he'd needed it and making it possible to learn the lessons of culture-driven selling, he made Mr. Stark his senior vice president of sales. Mr. Stark, in this new position, had greater insight into the company's records, systems, and numbers, and discovered an expense report falsification scheme headed by none other than Stuart Lame, who was escorted out of the building with his belongings in a box—permanently. Linda became Ralph's chief marketing officer. And Ralph hired David and his team to come in and help him run "The Culture-Driven Selling Program" to train the organization's nationwide sales team.

Ralph was able to also honor his former mentor, friend, and boss Sam by putting a special plaque in the Hall of Fame at all the plants and instituting a scholarship program for the employees in Sam's name—to honor his memory and to remind themselves that if they lost their way again, the wrong culture can demand the ultimate price.

About the Author

John Waid was born in Mexico City and started his business career unloading potato trucks in the manufacturing plant and as a route salesman for Frito-Lay in Mexico and the United States. His front-line experience and passion for the people on the front lines would never leave John. He continued his career in sales roles from the bottom up at Warner-Lambert (now Pfizer), IBM, PepsiCo, Nestle and Chateau Ste. Michelle winery.

John started as a human behavior consultant for one of the top European leadership training firms and became passionate about corporate culture and its importance as the number one focus of the greatest companies and leaders. John was inspired by the Peter Drucker quote, "Culture eats strategy for breakfast," and started his own firm, C3—Corporate Culture Consulting, to live the quote and work with leaders and their companies on their cultures. John is a son, husband, dad, CEO, trainer, author, and speaker and believes that people and corporate culture are the greatest competitive advantages in business. His vision is corporate culture in every company—C3.

John can be contacted at 404-915-3051 or jwaid@corporatecultureconsulting.com.

Acknowledgments

I would like to thank my mom, Priscilla, who loved people and inspired the compassion in me to help other people and employees, and my dad, John, who taught and guided me in my business career, which was cultivated and grew from the ground up. Their combined strengths coupled in me and led me to a lifelong journey to climb Culture Mountain in business and, most importantly, in life. Thanks, Mom and Dad, for the hard work, love, values, and behaviors you nurtured in me that helped me become the person I am.

I also want to thank Bill Skelton for the title *Reinventing Ralph*.

99758228R10081

Made in the USA
Columbia, SC
13 July 2018